D1371146

What Does God Do?

God Speaks to Children About His World

Text adapted from the
International Children's Bible
Illustrated by Hans Wilhelm

SP
Sweet Publishing
3934 Sandshell, Ft. Worth, TX 76137

Illustrations copyright © 1987 by Hans Wilhelm. Text adapted
from the *International Children's Bible*, copyright © 1986
by Sweet Publishing, Fort Worth, TX 76137.

Library of Congress Catalog Card Number 87-42782
ISBN 0-8344-0150-9

Concept: Carol Bartley
Design: Koechel/Peterson Design, Mpls., MN

10 9 8 7 6 5 4 3 2 1

A Word to the Reader

"Where does rain come from?" asks the small child.
"From the jars of heaven," answers God.
 Or so he says in Job.

Amid all the literal, scientific, adult explanations, God himself describes the world in a delightfully simple way. In whimsical passages from Job, Psalms and Isaiah, God paints vivid, childlike word pictures. Here is a God who cares about every detail of his universe, who takes the time to count the clouds and to water the desert. Here is a God who cares about each person and plans for him even before he is born. Here is a God who cares to communicate to a child's mind. Perhaps it was for the child—or the child in us all—that God included these passages in his holy Word.

Children will surely mature in their understanding of what makes it rain. But this book is dedicated to the hope that they will never outgrow their view of God as warm, loving and actively involved in the lives of his children.

God made
the earth's
foundation.

Job 38:4

He marked off how big it should be.

Job 38:5

He used scales
to weigh the
mountains
and hills.

Isaiah 40:12

God measured
the oceans
in the palm
of his hand.

Isaiah 40:12

He said to the sea,
"You may come this far,
but no farther.
This is where your
proud waves must stop."

Job 38:11

He stretches out the skies like a piece of cloth. He spreads them out like a tent to sit under.

Isaiah 40:22

God created all the stars.
He calls them all by name.
So not one of them
is missing.

Isaiah 40:26

He can tie up the stars of the Pleiades. He can loosen the ropes of the stars in Orion. He can bring out the stars at the right times.

Job 38:31, 32

He gives orders for the morning to begin and shows the dawn where its place is.

Job 38:12

He has the wisdom to count
the clouds and can pour
water from the jars of heaven.

Job 38:37

He waters the land where no one lives. He sends rain to satisfy the empty land so the grass begins to grow.

Job 38:26, 27

Have you ever gone into the storehouse where snow is kept? Or have you seen the storehouses for hail?

Job 38:22

God spreads the snow like wool. He scatters the frost like ashes.

Psalm 147:16

He hunts food
for the female lion
to satisfy the hunger
of the young lions.
He gives food
to cattle and to
the little birds
that call.

Job 38:39; Psalm 147:9

God commands the eagle to fly
and build his nest so high.
The eagle lives on a high cliff
and stays there at night.
From there he looks for food.
His eyes can see it
from far away.

Job 39:27-29

And God made your whole being.
He made you in an amazing
and wonderful way.

All the days planned for you
were written in his book
before you were one day old.

Psalm 139:13-16

I will speak using stories.
	I will tell things that have been secret
		since long ago.
We have heard them and know them.
	Our fathers told them to us.
We will not keep them from our children.
	We will tell those who come later
		about the praises of the Lord.
We will tell about his power
	and the miracles he has done.

Psalm 78:2-4

All scriptures are from the *International Children's Bible*.

TRI-CITIES CHRISTIAN SCHOOL
BRISTOL LOCATION